NATIONAL GEOGRAPHIC

EARTH SCIENCE

Extreme Weather

GLEN PHELAN

PICTURE CREDITS
Cover © Superstock. Page 1 © Michael S. Yamashita/
Corbis; pages 2–3 © Mike Hill/ImageState-Pictor/
PictureQuest; pages 4–5 © Merrilee Thomas/
Tom Stack & Associates; page 5 © Jim Reed/Corbis;
page 6 © 2001 Alan Moller; page 7 © Getty Images;
page 8 © Patti McConville/ImageState, pages 9, 11,
12, 14–15, 17 (top), 20, 26 © International Mapping
Associates; page 9 © Don Martel Photography;
pages 13, 25 © Tsado/NOAA/NCDC/Tom Stack &
Associates; page 16 © Dave Martin/Associated Press;
page 17 (lower) © Visum/A Vossberg/The Image
Works; page 18 © Wade Spees/The Post and Courier/
Associated Press; page 19 © Chuck Doswell/Painet Inc;
page 20 (inset) © Visuals Unlimited; page 21 (left)
© John Anderson/Earth Scenes; page 21(right)
© Corbis; page 22 © Don Lloyd/The Reporter/
Associated Press; page 23 Robert E. Barber; page 24
© NOAA photo library; page 27 (left) © V. Richard Haro/
Fort Collins Coloradoan/Associated Press; page 27
(right) © National Center for Atmospheric Research/
University Corporation for Atmospheric Research/
National Science Foundation; pages 28, 29 Sharon
Hoogstraten; page 31 © Mark Lewis /Mira.com.

Cover photo: Drought conditions near Wupertal, Germany

Produced through the worldwide resources of the National Geographic
Society, John M. Fahey, Jr., President and Chief Executive Officer; Gilbert
M. Grosvenor, Chairman of the Board; Nina D. Hoffman, Executive Vice
President and President, Books and Education Publishing Group.

PREPARED BY NATIONAL GEOGRAPHIC SCHOOL PUBLISHING
Ericka Markman, Senior Vice President and President, Children's Books
and Education Publishing Group; Steve Mico, Vice President, Editorial
Director; Rosemary Baker, Executive Editor; Barbara Seeber, Editorial
Manager; Jim Hiscott, Design Manager; Kristin Hanneman, Illustrations
Manager; Matt Wascavage, Manager of Publishing Services;
Sean Philpotts, Production Manager, Jane Ponton, Production Artist.

MANUFACTURING AND QUALITY MANAGEMENT
Christopher A. Liedel, Chief Financial Officer; Phillip L. Schlosser,
Director; Clifton M. Brown III, Manager.

PROGRAM DEVELOPER
Kate Boehm Jerome

ART DIRECTION
Daniel Banks, Project Design Company

CONSULTANT/REVIEWER
Dr. Timothy Cooney, Professor of Earth Science and Science Education,
University of Northern Iowa

BOOK DEVELOPMENT
Navta Associates

Published by the National Geographic Society
1145 17th Street, N.W.
Washington, D.C. 20036-4688

ISBN 0-7922-4575-X

Fourth printing November, 2005
Printed in Canada.

Contents

Twister!

Few sights are more awesome—
or frightening—than a tornado.

May 4, 2003, dawned bright and beautiful in much of the Midwest. But by late afternoon, swarms of tornadoes were tearing wildly through eight states.

The destruction was incredible. Among the sites worst hit was Pierce City, Missouri. Almost every building in this town of 1,400 people was destroyed or seriously damaged. Cars were flung around like toys. Huge trees snapped like twigs. Shards of wood became daggers hurled into the sides of houses.

The governor of Missouri called it "the most devastating series of tornadoes" the state had ever seen. More than 30 tornadoes, or twisters, carved deadly paths across the country's midsection. Over the next several days, that number would grow to more than 300—one of the worst outbreaks in history.

How did it happen? What weather events came together to produce such an awesome force of nature? More important, how successful are we at predicting such storms? That's what you're about to find out. Get ready for extreme weather!

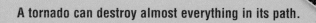

A tornado can destroy almost everything in its path.

Chapter 1

Stormy Weather

Raging Forces

A quiet Texas evening is about to get a lot more interesting. These massive storm clouds are producing torrential rain as well as hail, high winds, and tornadoes.

Storm clouds roll across the northern Texas plains.

Dry, cracked soil is one sign of drought.

W hat's the weather today? Would you describe it as extreme? Extreme weather includes conditions that endanger people's lives or damage property. That might mean intense winds or heavy rains. It could mean bitter cold, pounding hail, or a blinding snowstorm.

Chances are that you aren't experiencing any of this extreme weather right now. But it's not rare. At this moment a couple thousand thunderstorms are raging around the world, mostly in the tropics. On the other hand, some places in Africa are enduring a **drought**. These places have had no rain for months or even years.

Extremely dry conditions can lead to wildfires.

Weather's Toll

Extreme weather can have some surprising—and tragic—consequences. For example, in July 1995, high temperatures and lots of moisture in the air, or **humidity**, created a heat wave in the Midwest. About a thousand people died as a result. Most of the victims were elderly people who couldn't take the stress from the heat.

Just a year earlier, extreme winter temperatures throughout much of the United States were the lowest in more than a century. In Minnesota about a hundred people died from exposure to the cold, heart attacks from shoveling snow, or traffic accidents caused by the weather.

Extreme weather takes its toll on human life. But it can have other consequences, too. A blizzard can bring a bustling city to a halt for days. An ice storm can damage power lines, cutting off electricity to homes and businesses. During a drought, drinking water supplies can dry up. Dried-out vegetation becomes fuel for wildfires. During the drought of 1988, U.S. farmers lost billions of dollars in crops. More than five million acres burned, including large sections of Yellowstone National Park.

Formation of a Thunderstorm

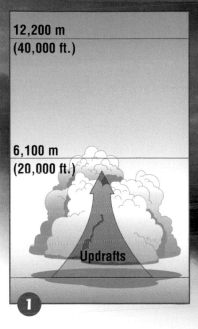

12,200 m
(40,000 ft.)

6,100 m
(20,000 ft.)

Updrafts

1

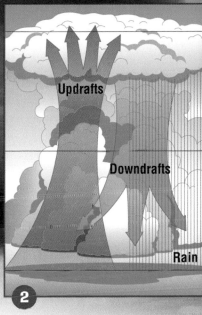

Updrafts

Downdrafts

Rain

2

1 Warm, moist air rises. The water vapor condenses and forms clouds. The rising air creates updrafts that bring more water vapor, and the cloud grows.

2 Water droplets and ice crystals become big enough to fall. They drag air down, forming downdrafts that bring pouring rain.

Storms on the Horizon

When you think of extreme weather, you probably think of thunderstorms and the severe weather they bring. Thunderstorms are heavy rainstorms that produce lightning and thunder. They form when warm, moist air rises rapidly. How can air be moist? All air contains some amount of **water vapor**, which is water in the form of a gas. The air in a thunderstorm has more water vapor than usual.

What makes the air rise? Think of a hot, muggy summer day. All day long the sun has been heating the ground. The warm ground warms the air above it. The heat makes the air particles move faster and farther apart. The air becomes lighter (less dense) and rises. As warm, moist air rises, it cools. As the air cools, its water vapor **condenses**, or changes into tiny droplets of liquid water and ice crystals. These droplets and crystals form a cloud.

Thunderheads

Warm, moist air also rises rapidly at a **cold front**. That's where a mass of cooler air bumps into a mass of warmer air. The cool air wedges under the warm air like a plow, pushing the warm air up sharply. A cloud grows quickly.

Whether the cloud forms at a cold front or not, upward movement of warm, moist air, or **updrafts**, feed the cloud. The cloud grows wider and higher. Then it becomes a huge thundering cloud, or a **thunderhead**. The water droplets and ice crystals become large enough to fall through the cloud, dragging air down with them. The ice crystals melt as they fall through warmer air. Rain pours down. (See the drawing on page 9.)

Flash . . . BOOM!

But rain is only part of the story. The thunderhead is now a violent system of updrafts and **downdrafts** moving at high speeds. This up-and-down air builds up positive and negative electric charges in the cloud. When the difference between these charges becomes great enough, **electrons** flow between them. This flow of electrons is a giant spark called lightning.

A lightning bolt heats the air to as much as 30,000°C (54,032°F). This intense, rapid heating makes the air expand explosively. The explosion is thunder. You see the lightning before you hear the thunder because light travels faster than sound.

Tornadoes

Perhaps the most frightening weather event of all is a tornado. A tornado is a funnel-shaped cloud of spinning, rising air. Tornadoes form during severe thunderstorms, especially in storms along a cold front.

Scientists think a tornado starts when crosswinds in a thunderhead blow at different speeds and in different directions. This action creates a horizontal spinning tube of air. Strong updrafts tilt the tube into a vertical funnel cloud. If the cloud touches the ground, it is called a tornado.

Low Pressure in Tornadoes

Tornadoes produce the fastest winds on Earth. The air inside the most powerful twisters spins more than 400 kilometers per hour (240 miles per hour). This speed is related to **air pressure**. Air pressure is the force of air pressing down on Earth's surface. Air moves from areas of high pressure to areas of low pressure. This movement of air is wind. The greater the difference is in air pressures, the faster the wind. The air pressure within a tornado is extremely low, so the tornado violently sucks in nearby air.

How a Tornado Works

Thundercloud

Sinking cool, dry air

Rising rotating current of warm, moist air

Direction of tornado

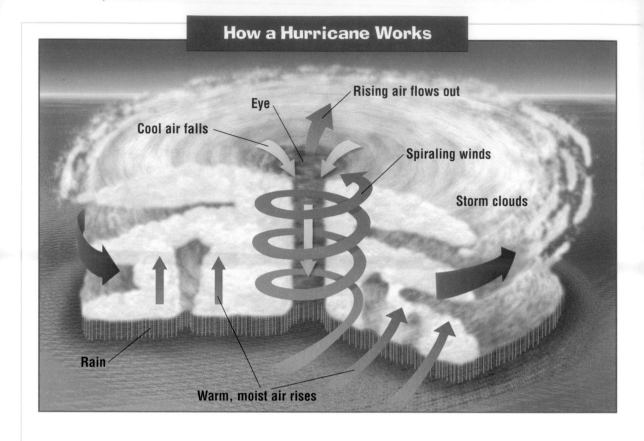

Rising air flows out

Eye

Cool air falls

Spiraling winds

Storm clouds

Rain

Warm, moist air rises

Hurricanes

You now know that all storms have warm, moist air. This type of air is common over the warm, tropical oceans near the Equator. It's not surprising, then, that the tropics are the starting points of the largest storms on Earth—hurricanes.

How does a hurricane form? Lots of water evaporates into the warm air above the tropical oceans. This warm, moist air rises, creating an area of low pressure. Warm air rushes into the area of low pressure to replace the air that is rising. Several thunderstorms form. The rotation of Earth causes the storms to clump together into one big storm and start turning like a huge pinwheel. Over several days the moving storm may grow to be several hundred miles across. As air pressure continues to fall in the center, the winds pick up speed. If the wind speed reaches 120 kilometers per hour (74 miles per hour), the storm is classified as a hurricane.

The Eye of the Storm

If you look at a satellite image of a hurricane, you probably notice two things: the swirling clouds and the circular center. This center is the storm's **eye**. The heaviest winds swirl in the cloud wall next to the eye. But the eye itself is an area of calm. In fact, sometimes the skies are clear. But that calm lasts only about a half hour at any one place as the giant, rotating storm slowly moves on. Then any place in the path of the storm gets socked with the cloud wall surrounding the eye.

Running Out of Energy

As long as the hurricane is positioned over warm water, it maintains its strength. But when it moves over land or over cooler water, it begins to lose its energy. The hurricane weakens, breaks up into separate thunderstorms, and then dies out.

The eye of a hurricane approaches the Florida coast.

Automated weather stations collect weather data around the clock, including temperature, humidity, air pressure, and more. But all this data means little unless it can be interpreted, or explained. That's one of the most important things a scientist does—**interpret data**.

For example, you know that storms are associated with areas of low pressure. The low pressure allows air to rise and clouds to form. Now suppose air pressure readings are rising. A scientist might interpret this data to mean that a mass of high-pressure air is moving into the area.

What kind of weather do you think high pressure would bring?

HINT **High pressure makes it difficult for air to rise.**

Mapping the Weather

How good are you at reading maps?
Once you understand what the
symbols mean, reading maps is a
breeze. Symbols on a weather map
have different lines, shapes, colors,
and numbers. Look at the symbols
in the key. What kind of weather
is shown for your hometown?

KEY

Hurricane

Rain

Thunderstorms

L Low pressure

H High pressure

Cold front (front edge
of cold air mass)

Warm front (front edge
of warm air mass)

Stationary front

— 1016 — Isobar (line connecting points of
equal air pressure, in millibars)

Temperature

−18	−12	−7	−1	4	10	16	21	27	32	38	°C

0	10	20	30	40	50	60	70	80	90	100	°F

Map labels: 1004, 1008, 1016, 1012, L

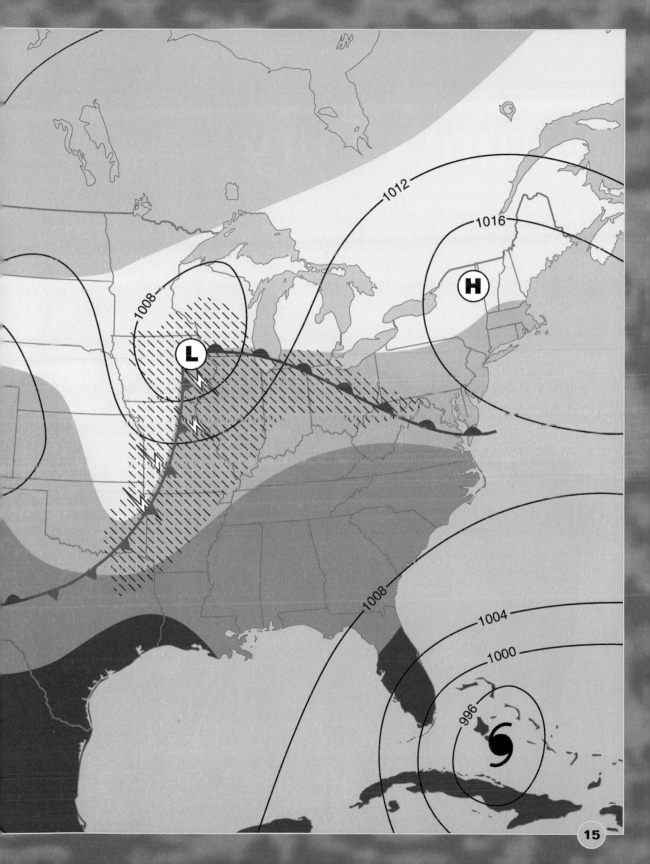

Chapter 2

Storm Hazards and Safety

Nature's Fury

The winds from a hurricane really pack a punch. But even greater dangers come with the floods that follow.

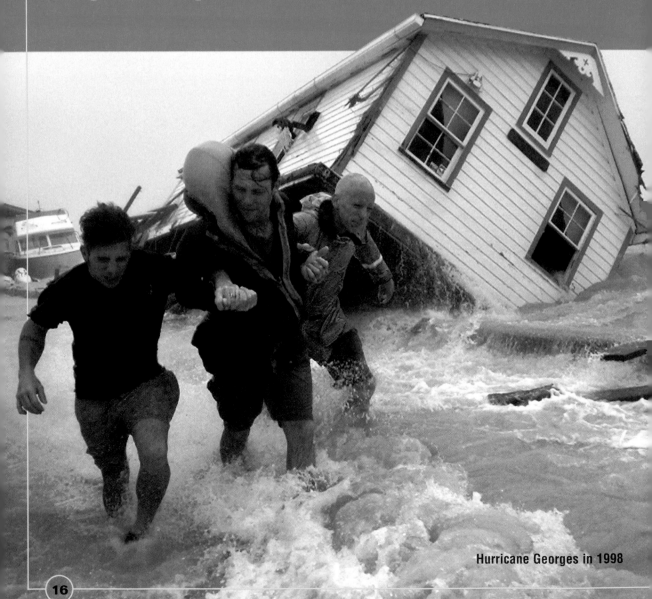

Hurricane Georges in 1998

Paths of Hurricanes

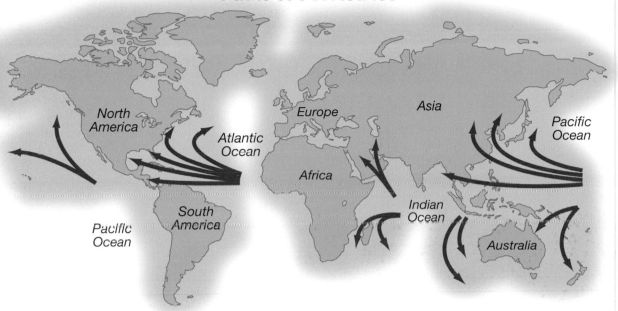

When a hurricane passes over an island or reaches a coastline, it can be devastating. Winds up to 360 kilometers per hour (220 miles per hour) rip trees from the ground and destroy buildings. To make matters worse, the spiraling bands of thunderheads often produce dozens of tornadoes.

The greatest loss of life, however, comes from raging floodwaters. Heavy rains can dump up to a foot of rain in just a few hours. The most destructive floods come from **storm surges.** A storm surge occurs as powerful winds push surface waters forward. This water piles up along the coast and washes over the land. On top of the storm surge, forceful winds create waves that can be as high as 12 meters (40 feet). Together, the storm surge and battering waves can demolish buildings and wipe out low-lying areas.

Hurricane Kyle in 2002 weakened into a tropical storm, but it still brought rains that flooded parts of Charleston, South Carolina.

Hurricane Safety

In 1900 a storm surge from a hurricane drowned about 10,000 people in Galveston, Texas. Today hurricanes are much less deadly. It's not that they are less powerful; it's that we can predict when they are coming.

By using satellites and other tools, forecasters can predict when and where a storm will hit land. When a hurricane is 36 hours away, the National Hurricane Center announces a hurricane watch.

People along the coast have time to board up windows, move boats to safer places, and make plans to **evacuate**, or leave the area.

The closer the storm gets to the coast, the more accurate the prediction becomes. When forecasters judge the hurricane to be 24 hours away, they issue a hurricane warning. Then people are urged to evacuate immediately.

Why do you think it is a good idea for people to evacuate when they get an official warning to do so?

"Like a Freight Train"

That's how people often describe the sound of an approaching tornado. The fierce roar of the whirling winds is something no one forgets. Neither is the damage the winds cause. Tornado damage is confined to the places where the funnel actually touches the ground. Some large tornadoes can leave a path of destruction half a mile wide.

The funnel cloud of a tornado is often dark gray. The color comes from the water vapor that condenses out of the air being pulled into the extreme low pressure area. But the funnel soon darkens from the soil and debris that get sucked into the whirling air. That debris—from stones to trees to bricks and glass to whole cars—is what causes most tornado injuries and deaths.

Soil and debris turn this funnel cloud black.

What if...?

. . . it started raining cats and dogs? Well, that's just a saying. But over the centuries, people around the world have reported other creatures raining from the sky during tornadoes and thunderstorms. Critters that have been sucked up and dropped by storms include frogs, fish, birds, and spiders. In 1968 the city of Acapulco, Mexico, received a shower of maggots!

Tornado Alley

More tornadoes strike the United States than any other country in the world. The United States averages about 800 twisters a year. Why? In the central United States cold, dry air from Canada meets warm, moist air from the Gulf of Mexico. Cold fronts form along this boundary, resulting in thunderstorms and tornadoes. In fact, the Great Plains states from Texas to North Dakota are part of an area called Tornado Alley. This area is especially active with tornadoes during the spring and early summer.

Tornado Safety

The National Weather Service issues a tornado watch if conditions are favorable for a tornado to form. If this happens in your area, you should prepare to take shelter. When the weather service spots a tornado, they issue a warning. At that time, sirens may sound in your community. It's time to seek shelter. Follow the safety tips shown at left.

Tornado Safety Tips

- Seek shelter in a basement or an interior room on the lowest level.

- Keep away from windows and doors.

- Get under a sturdy table, or use cushions to protect yourself from flying debris.

- Do not stay in mobile homes.

- Do not stay in vehicles.

- Seek shelter in a ditch if you can't get indoors.

Tornado Alley

North Dakota
South Dakota
Nebraska
Kansas
Oklahoma
Texas

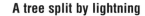

A tree split by lightning

When Lightning Strikes

If you don't live along the Gulf of Mexico or southeastern coast, you may not have experienced a hurricane. You may not have been in a tornado either, even if you live in Tornado Alley. But you have been in many thunderstorms. The greatest danger of these storms comes from lightning.

Each year in the United States lightning causes thousands of forest fires. It knocks out electrical power during many severe storms. It kills about a hundred people a year and injures hundreds more. The safety tips at right offer some ways to avoid the dangers of lightning.

Lightning Safety Tips

- Go indoors during thunderstorms.
- Stay away from open windows and doors.
- Do not touch appliances, electrical cords, or metal plumbing.
- Do not use the phone.
- If you are in water, get out immediately.
- If you are caught in an open area outdoors, crouch down and bend forward to make yourself as small a target as possible for lightning.
- If you are outdoors, do not seek shelter under a tree.

Chapter 3

Predicting Storms

High-Tech Detection

Awesome! Tim Samaras sits in his vehicle and watches the twister heading straight for him. 300 yards away . . . 200 yards . . . 150 yards. . .

When the tornado is about 100 yards (90 meters) away, Tim jumps out of the van, drops a cone-shaped object on the ground, and speeds off. Only 80 seconds later, the twister passes over the spot and sucks the cone up into its whirling winds. Tim sees the whole thing and couldn't be happier. It's history in the making.

Storm Chasers

Tim Samaras is a **storm chaser**. Storm chasers are scientists or researchers who follow severe thunderstorms and the tornadoes they can produce. Storm chasers use a variety of instruments to gather data about thunderstorms and tornadoes. This information helps scientists understand how tornadoes form and how to more accurately predict them.

Tim Samaras with his turtle probe

The object Tim placed in the tornado's path is a probe called a turtle. It's packed with sensors that measure wind speed, wind direction, air pressure, temperature, and humidity. When the twister hit the probe on June 24, 2003, it was a first—the first time that all these factors were measured in the same tornado. The probe, which Tim helped design, also measured the biggest drop in air pressure ever recorded between the outside and inside of a tornado.

VORTEX

The information Tim collected is especially interesting to Erik Rasmussen, a scientist and fellow storm chaser. In 1994 and 1995, Erik directed the largest storm chase ever. It was called the Verification of the Origins of Rotation in Tornadoes Experiment (VORTEX). It's a fitting name because a vortex is the center of a tornado. VORTEX included more than 100 researchers, 2 planes, and 21 vehicles loaded with instruments.

Erik and his team traveled the Tornado Alley states of Texas, Oklahoma, and Kansas. Did they just roam the plains hoping to come across a twister? Hardly.

Like other storm researchers, they used satellite images and computers to find and track **supercells**. These are the largest, most dangerous thunderstorms, and they can spin out one tornado after another. The photo on page 6 shows part of a supercell.

The Dimmitt Tornado

VORTEX was an exciting project. But no one could have predicted just how exciting it would get. On June 2, 1995, during the last week of the project, researchers were studying a supercell near Dimmitt, Texas. Suddenly, the thunderhead spawned a powerful tornado. The storm chasers sprang into action.

Armed with storm-chasing technology, VORTEX researchers hit the road.

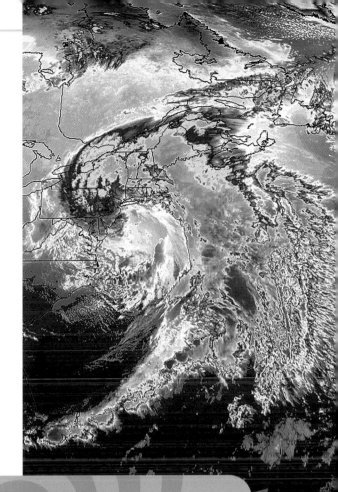

Doppler radar images of a storm hitting the northeastern coast of the U.S.

Some vehicles moved ahead of the storm. They launched balloons carrying instruments that measured pressure, humidity, and temperature at different altitudes. Other vehicles spread out under the thunderhead, taking measurements. A **Doppler radar** mounted on a truck recorded the entire ten-minute life of the tornado, providing pictures of its wind speed and direction. Two planes with Doppler radar also gathered data.

A Busy Future

The Dimmitt tornado became the most observed twister in history. Scientists are still analyzing the data collected from it. All together, VORTEX has gathered data on 31 thunderstorms. This information helps scientists learn why some storms produce tornadoes and others do not. Every year, scientists get closer to unlocking the mysteries of this incredible force.

Stay Tuned!

A radar system used by the U.S. Navy is being tested for weather prediction. Called phased array radar, it scans a storm in one minute instead of the five to six minutes required with current Doppler radars. It also measures rapid changes in wind that cannot be measured with Doppler. The new system should increase warning times for severe weather and make predictions more accurate.

Interpreting Data

Suppose the air pressure in your area is steadily falling. It's warm and humid, but air coming from the west is cooler and drier. The winds are beginning to shift direction. What does it all mean?

Interpreting data is a big part of any scientist's job. It's especially important for predicting the weather.

Weather data are collected over a wide area. Arranging the data on maps makes it easier to see patterns and tell what the data mean.

The map below shows a section of the United States that is experiencing a change in the weather. The arrows show the wind direction around the low pressure area.

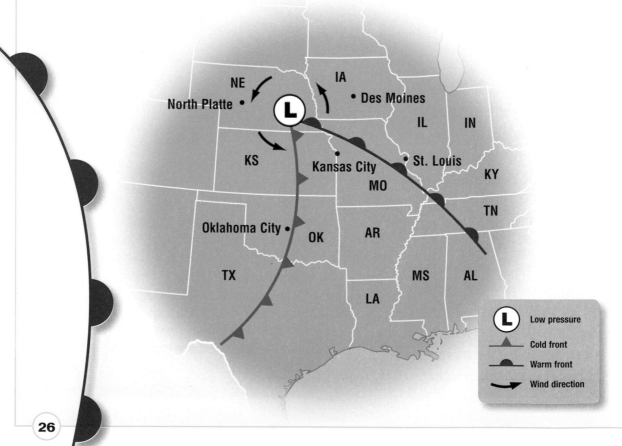

Practice the Skill

Answer the following questions to interpret the data that are shown on the map.

1. What is about to happen to the temperature of the air in St. Louis? How do you know?

2. From which direction is the wind blowing in North Platte?

3. The low is expected to be over southern Illinois a day later. What do you think the weather in Oklahoma City will be like then?

Check It Out

Which city on the map do you think is experiencing the weather conditions described in the first paragraph on page 26? Why do you think this?

Fun With Air Pressure

You know that air moves from areas of high pressure to areas of low pressure. This movement of air feeds storms and helps produce tornadoes and hurricanes. Want to see some other things that differences in air pressure can do? Try these "tricks" on family and friends.

Materials
- ✔ Plastic sandwich bag
- ✔ Wide-mouthed jar
- ✔ Plastic cup
- ✔ Index card
- ✔ Table tennis ball
- ✔ Plastic funnel

SAFETY TIP: When working with liquids, wipe up any spills immediately.

Explore

Heavy Bag

1 Place a sandwich bag inside a jar. Lap the top of the bag over the jar rim. *(See photograph A.)*

2 Press the bag against the inside of the jar so that there is as little air as possible between the jar and the bag.

3 Hold the bag tightly around the rim with your hands. Have someone grab the inside bottom of the bag and try to pull it out of the jar.

The bag doesn't come out because the air pressing down on the inside of the bag is a lot greater than the little bit of air that is pressing up under the bag between the bag and the jar.

B

Magic Card

1 In a sink or over a plastic container, fill a plastic cup to overflowing with water. You don't want any air between the top of the water and the rim of the cup.

2 Place an index card over the top of the cup. Keep one hand on the card as you flip the cup over. Then, let go of the card. *(See photograph B.)*

The water doesn't flow out because there is so little air in the cup. The air pressure inside the cup is very low. Therefore the air pressure outside the cup is higher than inside the cup. The air pushes up on the card enough to hold the water in place.

Ball That Defies Gravity

1 Place a table tennis ball inside a funnel. Turn the funnel so that the large opening faces down. Hold the ball in place so that it doesn't fall out.

2 Blow hard into the small end of the funnel. Let go of the ball. As long as you continue blowing, the ball will float within the funnel.

The ball stays in the funnel because the faster air moves over a surface, the less pressure it exerts on that surface. So when you blow air over the ball, an area of low pressure is created above the ball. The air pressure pushing up on the bottom of the ball is now greater, and that keeps the ball floating.

Think

Suppose you blow up two balloons, tie each of them to a separate piece of string, and hold them by the strings so that they are a couple inches apart. If you blow air between the balloons, in which direction do you think they will move? Try it. Can you explain your observations?

HINT As air moves faster, its pressure decreases.

SAFETY TIP: Be sure to wear safety goggles when you work with balloons.

Science Notebook

STORM FACTS

- You can tell how far away lightning is by counting the number of seconds between the lightning and the thunder. Divide that number of seconds by 3 to get the distance in kilometers. (Divide by 5 for the distance in miles.)

- The first hurricane of the year is given a name beginning with A. The second one begins with a B, and so on. The names switch between male and female. Names can be used again after six years.

- On January 23, 1916, the temperature in Browning, Montana, was 7°C (44°F). The next day it was –49°C (–56°F). That's a 56°C (100°F) difference, the biggest one-day temperature swing ever.

- In April 1921, 193 centimeters (76 inches) of snow fell on Silver Lake, Colorado, in one 24-hour period—a North American record.

BOOKS TO READ

Allaby, Michael. *Guide to Weather: A Photographic Journey Through the Skies*. Dorling Kindersley, 2000. Amazing photographs reveal the awesome power of Earth's extreme weather.

Christian, Spencer, and Antonia Felix. *Can It Really Rain Frogs? The World's Strangest Weather Events*. John Wiley & Sons, 1997. Fascinating facts and fun activities help you explore our wild, wacky weather.

Lye, Keith. *The Weather Atlas*. Running Press, 2001. Colorful diagrams and photographs help explain the weather around the globe.

WEBSITES TO VISIT

Storm Prediction Center
www.spc.noaa.gov

University of Nebraska-Lincoln High Plains Regional Climate Center
www.hprcc.unl.edu/nebraska/
U_S_SEVERE.html

Glossary

air pressure – the force of air pressing down on Earth's surface

cold front – the boundary of a cold air mass that is pushing out a warm air mass

condense – to change from a gas into a liquid

Doppler radar – a tool that shows the movement of winds in a storm

downdraft – a downward movement of air

drought (*DROUT*) – a long period of time with little or no rain or snow

electron (*i-LEK-tron*) – a particle of matter that has a negative charge

evacuate (*i-VAK-yoo-ayt*) – to leave an area in an organized way for safety reasons

eye – the calm region in the center of a hurricane

humidity – a measure of the amount of water vapor in the air

interpret data – to explain information

meteorologist (*mee-tee-uh-RAHL-uh-jist*) – a scientist who studies Earth's atmosphere and the weather

storm chaser – a researcher who follows severe thunderstorms to study them

storm surge – a mass of water pushed on land by winds during a hurricane

supercell – a large thunderstorm that produces the strongest tornadoes

thunderhead – a large cloud that produces lightning, thunder, and heavy rains

updraft – an upward movement of air

water vapor – water in the form of a gas

Index